A GUIDE TO THE STATE'S NORTHWEST CORNER

WASHINGTON
in your pocket

OTHER BOOKS BY KIKI CANNIFF

WASHINGTON FREE – A Guide to the Best of the State's
Cost Free Attractions

FREE CAMPGROUNDS OF WASHINGTON & OREGON

OREGON FREE – A Guide to the Best of the State's Cost Free
Attractions

OREGON'S FREE CAMPGROUNDS

SAUVIE ISLAND; A STEP BACK IN TIME

A GUIDE TO THE STATE'S NORTHWEST CORNER

WASHINGTON
in your pocket

By KiKi Canniff

Illustrations by Janora Bayot

Ki² Enterprises
P.O. Box 13322
Portland, OR 97213

Library of Congress Cataloging-in-Publication Data

Canniff, KiKi, 1948–
    Washington in your pocket.

    Includes index.
    1. Washington (State)--Description and travel--
1981-   --Guide-books. I. Title.
F889.3.C37 1986   917.97'70443   86-7225
ISBN 0-9608744-7-X

ISBN #0-9608744-7-X

Ki² Enterprises
P.O. Box 13322
Portland, OR 97213

TABLE OF CONTENTS

6

INTRODUCTION

WASHINGTON IN YOUR POCKET will show you the very best of what Washington's northwest corner has to offer. Areas covered include most of Whatcom, Skagit, Island and Snohomish Counties, plus Seattle and the Upper Olympic Peninsula.

This corner holds some of the state's most popular attractions including the upper portion of the beautiful Cascade Loop, awesome Mt. Baker, the famed San Juan Islands, North Cascades and Olympic National Parks, plus protected wilderness beaches, luxurious rain forests, historically restored pioneer towns, museums, special activities, hiking trails and a whole lot more.

If you're arriving from Canada your port of entry will most likely be Blaine, via Canadian Highway 99/U.S. I-5, or Port Angeles, on the ferry from Victoria. Both routes will take you to a number of exciting attractions.

This book was designed with those two ports of entry in mind. Our first section begins at Blaine, the second at Port Angeles. However, it is also easy to access this book in reverse, starting with Seattle or any other northwest corner city.

WASHINGTON IN YOUR POCKET is also perfect for everyone who lives in or near the northwest corner. It tells you about nearly 200 places you can enjoy with your family while exploring the unmatched beauty of Washington's northwest corner.

WASHINGTON'S NORTHWEST CORNER

VANCOUVER B.C.

CANADIAN–UNITED STATES BORDER

BLAINE

LYNDEN

FERNDALE

NORTH CASCADES PARK

BELLINGHAM

BAKER LAKE

ANACORTES

CONCRETE

NEWHALEM

BURLINGTON

SAN JUAN ISLANDS

LA CONNER

SNOQUALMIE NATIONAL FOREST

WHIDBY ISLAND

DARRINGTON

MARYSVILLE

SNOHOMISH

PUGET SOUND

N

SEATTLE

13

Blaine is known as *The Peace Arch City*. It is right at the U.S. border and is the last stop for anyone entering Canada via I–5. Its border station is open 24 hours a day.

Peace Arch Park is situated right on the international boundary between Canada and the United States. It was named for the towering Peace Arch built there in 1921 with pennies donated by American and Canadian school children and commemorates the lasting peace between our two great nations.

This beautifully landscaped park is maintained jointly by Washington and British Columbia. One half of the arch rests in each country. On the U.S. side it reads "Children Of a Common Mother" the Canadian face proclaims "Brethren Dwelling Together in Unity". Rhododendrons, azaleas, heather and more than 27,000 annual flowers provide bright color, particularly during July and August. Each year, on the second Sunday in June, this lovely park becomes the site of the International Peace Arch Celebration where the two nations join together in celebration of peaceful co-existence.

Birch Bay and **Birch Bay State Park** are about six miles south of Blaine. Visitors here will see remnants of Indian shellfish beds and huge fir stumps left behind by early area loggers. The bay offers warm water swimming bordered by 193 acres of Puget Sound shoreline, marshes and forests. Clamming, crabbing, beachcombing, scuba diving, water skiing, shore fishing, picnicking and camping can all be enjoyed here. Visitors may also be treated to a glimpse of beavers, opossums, muskrats or any of 300 species of birds, including the Great Blue Heron, at its small estuary.

Park hours are 6:30 a.m. to 10:00 p.m. April 1 to October 15 and 8:00 a.m. to 5:00 p.m. October 16 through March 31. You'll find the park three miles off the I-5 freeway at 5105 Helwig Road in Birch Bay.

Semiahmoo Spit was the site of an Indian trading post during the 19th century. Today visitors will find a park, marina and museum where carefully restored historic buildings are nestled in a setting of natural beauty. The interpretive center reveals Semiahmoo's heritage and maritime history. Outside, the park offers picnicking, beachcombing, swimming, and what is said to be some of the best bird watching in the country.

To reach Semiahmoo Spit exit I-5 to Birch Bay-Lynden Road, turn west to Harbor View Road, turn left to Birch Bay Drive, then right to Birch Point Road and continue to Semiahmoo Drive and the park entrance.

Lynden is a few miles east of Blaine in the fertile Nooksack River Valley. It is also reached via the Birch Bay-Lynden Road. Each year Lynden is the site of an **international horse-drawn plowing match** using Percheron and Clydesdale draft horses. This authentic match claims to be the only meet of its kind held west of the Mississippi River. It always happens on the first Saturday in June.

The Puget Sound Antique Tractor and Machinery Association also sponsors an **old-fashioned threshing bee** here each summer. This event takes place over a four day period, ending on the first Saturday in August, and features the largest display of old tractors and farm machinery on the West Coast.

Many events are held in conjunction with both of these two displays. A complete schedule is available from the Lynden Chamber of Commerce, (206) 354-5995.

The **Lynden Pioneer Museum** is located at the intersection of Third and Front Streets. The large brick building it is housed in was built around 1910 and once served as a blacksmith shop.

The items displayed here include a forty piece collection of antique buggies, wagons, carts and other horse-drawn vehicles bequeathed to the city by Fred K. Polinder, a long time resident. Summer hours are 10:00 a.m. to 4:00 p.m. Monday thru Saturday. During the winter they are only open on Thursdays, Fridays and Saturdays.

South of Blaine along I-5 you'll find **Ferndale**, a picturesque little city built along the banks of the Nooksack River. This river harbors salmon, steelhead and cutthroat trout.

Ferndale is the site of Whatcom County's historic **Hovander Homestead Park**. Here, in 1897 Holan Hovander selected for his home a farm site boasting one mile of Nooksack River frontage. He painstakingly laid the brick foundations for the house himself. The house has been restored to its turn-of-the century elegance and is open to the public. Most of the antique furnishings were brought by the Hovanders from Sweden or collected by Holan's son Otis.

It is easy for visitors to this park to visualize what a working farm was like in the early twentieth century. The huge red barn has been restored and houses a fine collection of farm implements used in the early days. In the tool shed you'll find a wide variety of old tools, harnesses and ropes. The milk house has also been restored and equipped with many of the instruments used by the Hovanders when making butter and cheese.

Summer hours for those wishing to tour the buildings are noon to 8:00 p.m. weekdays and 10:00 a.m. to 8:00 p.m. Saturdays, Sundays and holidays. Winter hours are 10:00 a.m. to 6:00 p.m. Saturdays, Sundays and holidays only. The park grounds are open to the public daily from dawn to dark, year round.

To reach the park take Hovander Road south out of Ferndale to Nielson Road, continue to River Lea Road, then on to the park.

Bellingham is the state's seventh largest city and a quick 20 minute drive south of the Canada/U.S. border. Boaters and sailors find the waters of Bellingham Bay and the adjoining San Juan Archipelago among the most beautiful and challenging in the world.

Hidden within the Bellingham city limits are remnants of the four original towns settled here on Bellingham Bay. The most colorful, Fairhaven, was conceived by a smuggler called Dirty Dan and originally the bay's main port. You can easily find **Old Fairhaven** by taking exit 250 off I–5 and heading towards the water. Twelfth Street was once Fairhaven's main street. You'll find three antique rail cars at Twelfth and Mill and a number of historic buildings in the surrounding blocks.

Western Washington University is located on the hill above Old Fairhaven. Its **Outdoor Sculpture Museum** started with just one piece in 1960. Today it contains the works of 16 artists. You can stretch your legs among the stone animals, rock rings, steaming rocks, log ramps leading nowhere and other astonishing outdoor artworks that dot the campus. Before you begin, stop at the drive-up visitors center on College Way for a map. They also put out a booklet explaining each of the pieces.

Sehome Hill is a native plant arboretum near campus that is jointly owned by Western Washington University and the city of Bellingham. This area was once counted among the world's most magnificent coniferous forests. Giant cedars, hemlocks and Douglas firs occupied all of the Bellingham townsite and its surrounding land. Many were over 12 feet in diameter and towered far above the abundant mosses, ferns and flowering plants of the area. Frontier lumbermen soon reduced the great trunks to lumber making way for civilization.

Protected as an arboretum, the hill has begun a centuries-long progression which should lead once again to a stable community of plants dominated by giant cedars, Douglas firs and hemlocks. Several miles of trails exist here and can be accessed from the parking lot near the top of the hill. The trails have names like Douglas Fir Lane, Sword Fern Lane, and Alder Walkway.

The **Whatcom Museum of History and Art** at 121 Prospect Street is one of the finest regional museums on the West Coast. Its building is listed on the National Register of Historic Landmarks and considered one of the few remaining examples of late Victorian civic architecture. It was built in 1892 and originally served as city hall for the town of New Whatcom, a decade before the city of Bellingham was formed. It has been beautifully restored.

On the first floor you will find five galleries where continually changing exhibits display art and/or history. The second floor contains three turn of the century rooms furnished to portray the influence of Queen Victoria's England on the United States. The Rotunda Room, originally a court room, usually features works by regional and nationally known artists. Off the Rotunda Room is the Collector's Case. This small area is regularly filled with some fascinating private collection.

The third floor offers permanent displays on Indian art and culture utilizing artifacts found from here northward to the Aleutian Islands. Early area logging is the subject of another display. The museum also has an extensive ornithology collection which includes more than 500 birds.

In 1923 **Larrabee State Park** became Washington's first official state park. Today, it encompasses 1,886 acres and includes 3,600 feet of shoreline along Samish Bay. With each changing of the tide its saltwater shoreline allows visitors to witness the intricate workings of its unique environment. Park tidal pools often exhibit several varieties of starfish, crabs, barnacles, sea cucumbers, chitons, limpets, mussels and fish. They offer a wonderful opportunity for children and adults to touch and observe these creatures as long as they then return them to their natural surroundings.

In addition to exploring sea life, visitors can hike the many trails or visit one of several mountain lookouts. These offer panoramic views of the San Juan Islands, Mount Baker and the North Cascade Mountains. Picnicking, camping, swimming, boating, fishing and scuba diving are other activities popular with park visitors. A saltwater boat launch is also available.

Larrabee State Park sits on the seaward side of Chuckanut Mountain, seven miles south of Bellingham on State Highway 11.

Silver Lake Park also offers a variety of activities. Swimming, fishing, camping, boating, picnicking and hiking are popular here. You can also learn about the area's past through its historical museum. This 411 acre park is operated by Whatcom County and offers full use from Memorial Day to Labor Day but limited use during the balance of the year. To reach it you must leave Bellingham on the Mt. Baker Highway heading for Maple Falls. From there you turn north on Silver Lake Road and follow the signs. It's about 3 miles to the park.

Samish Park is also county operated. It was once the site of a log rafting pond and fishing resort. Today, visitors will find hiking trails, picnic tables and a children's play area. Fishing, swimming and boating are popular too with pedal boats, row boats and canoes being available for rental. You'll find everything open from Memorial Day to Labor Day but limited use the balance of the year. To reach the park leave I-5 on North Lake Samish Drive. You'll find this exit just south of Bellingham. Follow this road west to the park.

Bellingham has a number of city parks too. Whatcom Falls Park is one of the largest with 241 acres. It's east of town on Lake Whatcom. Lake Padden Park lies to the south and includes over 1000 acres and a swimming beach. You'll find rose gardens at Cornwall and Fairhaven Parks. Fairhaven is at 107 Chuckanut Drive; Cornwall at 2800 Cornwall Avenue.

Railroad buffs will want to ride the authentic steam powered train that operates between Wickersham and Lake Whatcom. The **Lake Whatcom Railway** operates only during June, July and August on Tuesdays and Saturdays. The 79-year old steamer takes you on a short ride through forests and farmlands. Tickets can be purchased at both the Wickersham and Lake Whatcom boarding areas, the round trip takes two hours. The railway also runs "speeders" on a track right on Lake Whatcom. These speeders operate between 10:00 a.m. and 5:00 p.m.; the steam engine leaves Wickersham at noon and 2:00 p.m. Wickersham is southeast of Bellingham, off the tip of Lake Whatcom.

Mount Baker, east of Bellingham, is what is known as a dormant volcano. Although normally quiet, it occasionally lets loose a burst of steam, much to the delight of those with cameras handy. A drive up the Mt. Baker Highway to the foothills affords an ever-changing panorama of mountains, forests and small towns.

The foothills offer year round activities. Skiing, snowmobiling, horseback riding, swimming, hiking, golfing and camping are all done here, in the shadow of this 10,778 foot peak. Mt. Baker is part of the Glacier Ranger District in the Mt. Baker-Snoqualmie National Forest. This forest is heavily timbered with fir, spruce, hemlock, and cedar. Wildlife includes elk, deer, bear and mountain goat plus numerous smaller forest animals.

Two of the best places for viewing Mt. Baker are Artist Point, 23 miles east of Glacier at the end of the Mt. Baker Highway and **Mt. Baker Viewpoint**. Artist Point is usually only accessible in August and September. The Mt. Baker Viewpoint is more accessible and found 9 miles up Glacier Creek Road. This road is less than a mile east of the town of Glacier. The viewpoint offers picnic tables as well as a spectacular view.

Hikers will enjoy **Damfino Lakes** and **Canyon Ridge Trails**. Two miles east of the Glacier Ranger Station turn left just beyond Douglas Fir Campground. This one spot provides access to both trails. For additional trail information stop in at the Ranger Station. They can direct you to trails just right for your skills and time.

Nooksack Falls is easily accessible too, simply take the Mt. Baker Highway 7 miles east of the Ranger Station to Wells Creek Road. The 170 foot waterfall is .5 mile up this road. If you follow that same road an additional 2–4 miles you may get a chance to see some of the mountain goats that live on Barometer Mountain. From the road they appear as tiny cream-colored blotches on the rock, binoculars or a high powered camera lens are necessary for a good look. The best time to see the goats is in the spring, just as the snow is melting. About 5 miles from the highway you will find a small waterfall on Wells Creek. The end of the road is an additional 5 miles and offers views of Mt. Baker and Lasiocarpa Ridge.

You must travel 13 miles east of the Ranger Station to Road 3071 to find the **Anderson Creek Beaver Dams**. Take this road 1.5 miles to where these industrious animals have built an extensive system of dams and created a marshy environment. The Pacific Northwest was once overrun with beavers. Today, only a few are lucky enough to catch a glimpse of this elusive animal.

I-5 may be the quickest route between Bellingham and **Burlington** but Highway 11, **Chuckanut Drive**, is the prettiest. It will take you past Samish Bay, Larrabee State Park and the thickly forested Chuckanut Mountain. Roadside viewpoints expose sweeping vistas of the beautiful San Juan Islands. You may even be treated to the sight of a killer whale amongst the islands or feeding seals in the tidal flats of Samish Bay.

If you take Highway 20 east out of Burlington you will be heading for the mountains and Washington's famed **Cascade Loop**. This loop drive winds through five river valleys and tops the Cascade Mountains at two different points offering some of the finest scenery available anywhere. The entire loop covers more than 400 miles. Roads utilized include Highway 20 from Anacortes to Twisp, Highway 153 from Twisp to Pateros, Highway 97 from Pateros to Wenatchee and Highway 2 from Wenatchee to Everett. Each new turn reveals the beauty of this high mountain area. Much of the surrounding land is public land, offering visitors a wealth of natural attractions.

For those who can't make the entire 400 mile loop the trip has been divided into four sections. The first section travels only Highway 20 and covers everything between Burlington and the 5,477 foot high Washington Pass. It is approximately 100 miles in length. Sedro Woolley, Concrete, Rockport, Marblemount, Newhalem, and Diablo are all located in between. This stretch is well worth seeing even if you can't make the entire loop.

The first town you encounter, 6 miles east of Burlington, is **Sedro Woolley**. Sedro is a Spanish word for the cedar trees that were once so abundant in the valley and the name given to an 1884 community on the banks of the Skagit River. Woolley was a sawmill community located a short distance inland. Growth soon united the two communities and their names.

Sedro Woolley is the gateway to the scenic North Cascade Mountains, the North Cascades National Park and Mt. Baker National Forest. The **Skagit River**, once a highway for sternwheelers, is popular with boaters, canoeists, rafters and nature lovers. The river's fighting steelhead, salmon and trout make it inviting to people who fish as well.

Approximately 157 miles of the Skagit, Sauk, Cascade and Suiattle Rivers are protected by the Federal **Wild and Scenic Rivers** Act. This includes 58 miles of the Skagit east of Sedro Woolley which is classified recreational. A recreational river is readily accessible by road and may have some development along the shoreline. The other three rivers all drain into the Skagit and are classified as scenic. A scenic river must be free of impoundments and have undeveloped shorelines.

Concrete is 23 miles east of Sedro Woolley and located in the center of one of the continental United States' most primitive mountain areas. It's a terrific starting point for those who like to get off the beaten path.

The **Baker Lake Recreation Area** offers spectacular scenery, towering mountain peaks, broad deep valleys, unique geological areas, historic sites and nature trails. Swimming, fishing, boating, sailing, water skiing, camping, hiking and mountain backpacking are all popular here. The road to Baker Lake leaves Highway 20 just before you reach Concrete. It will take you north for about 14 miles before reaching the **Mt. Baker-Snoqualmie National Forest** boundary and Baker Lake. Three miles further you'll find a forest service guard station where visitors can get up-to-date recreational information during the summer. The balance of the year you can stop at the forest service headquarters just east of Birdsview, before following the road to Baker Lake.

Well maintained forest roads allow you to choose from a number of interesting side trips and give you plenty of opportunities to stretch your legs or just sit quietly and enjoy a picnic lunch. Blue Lake Road will treat you to panoramic views of Mt. Baker, Mt. Shuksan, Mt. Blum, Mt. Watson, Welker Peak and Baker Lake as well as access to the Blue Lake trailhead. This trail takes you through pleasant mountain meadows for an .8 mile jaunt to Blue Lake. Lucky visitors may catch a glimpse of the magnificent Roosevelt elk that summer here.

Another good trail is the **Shadow of the Sentinels Nature Trail**. It contains one of the most beautiful stands of old growth Douglas fir left in this area. Many of the trees are estimated to be over 600 years old.

At the south end of Baker Lake, near the dam, is the Glover Mountain Observation Point. It offers a view of Baker Dam and nearby Lake Shannon plus a short nature hike. Lake Shannon is one of the few places where osprey, an uncommon species of hawk, are often sighted.

Concrete is also home to the **North Cascades National Park** information center. Photos and displays found here will help to answer any questions you have about the area. This park is sometimes referred to as the American Alps, covers 1,053 square miles and harbors 318 glaciers. Hiking, backpacking and mountaineering are the most popular activities in the park. Trails lead to views of glacially sculpted valleys, high mountain glaciers, flower filled meadows and glimmering white snowfields. The North Cascades Highway provides access to all of its wonders.

Rockport is 9 miles east of Concrete and right next door to the 1,500 acre **Skagit River Bald Eagle Natural Area**. This is the primary wintering ground for approximately 300 northern bald eagles. A number of designated parking and vista areas have been established to allow for viewing without disturbing the eagles.

Bald eagles are easiest to spot during early morning or late afternoon when they search the river bars for salmon, especially during spawning season. On snowy or rainy windless days they often perch patiently above their feeding sites through mid-day hours. Bald eagles are an endangered species and protected by law. It is this protection which has established the Skagit River Bald Eagle Natural Area as a critical roosting, nesting, perching and feeding site.

Rockport State Park protects a stand of Douglas fir that is several hundred years old and nearly 300 feet in height. This land was first settled by the Skagit Indians. They built their village of long houses at the confluence of the Sauk and Skagit Rivers. The park offers 5 miles of foot trails, including Sauk Springs Trail which is suitable for wheelchairs.

For an overall view of the area take the 7.5 mile gravel road just west of the park to the top of Sauk Mountain. For an even more spectacular view hike the 1.5 mile trail. Your reward will be a vista which includes the North Cascade Range, the Skagit and Sauk River Valleys, Mt. Baker and Puget Sound.

Steelhead Park is located along one of the Skagit River's best fishing areas. It yields steelhead and various types of salmon. The park has a wonderful history collection. First there's the historic Porter log cabin. Built in 1884, the timbers of this cabin were hand-hewn and the corners dove-tailed so that no framing or nails were required. The Rockport Ferry also occupies a place of honor, overlooking the stretch of water it crossed so many times. It was retired in 1961. A dugout canoe once belonging to Chief Campbell is on display too. A boat launch and picnic facilities are among the amenities offered here.

Your journey eastward is taking you ever higher into this beautifully mountainous country. **Marblemount** is 9 miles east of Rockport. In the 1880's this town was crowded with miners who had flocked into the Upper Skagit River Valley in search of gold. The old Marblemount Hotel and the Log House Inn are two of the towns original buildings. This area offers hikers ten different **trails** to choose from. Some lead into well traveled areas, others into the wilderness. One mile off Highway 20, in Marblemount, you can visit the North Cascades National Park's district headquarters for trail information and overnight backpacking permits.

One mile southeast of town, on the Rockport-Cascade Road, the **Skagit Salmon Hatchery** welcomes visitors. They have 20 ponds and 4 rearing channels in operation. King, silver and chum salmon are raised here.

Newhalem is 14 miles east of Marblemount; Diablo an additional 7 miles. Newhalem offers two self-guided **walking tours** for visitors. The Ladder Creek Falls Trail passes a series of waterfalls and takes you through a garden of rhododendrons, maidenhair ferns and countless varieties of trees. It is lighted at night, throughout the summer, and can be found behind Gorge Powerhouse. The second, Trail of the Cedars, will take you on a short walk where area plant and wildlife are explained. The trail ends at the historic Newhalem Powerhouse.

Diablo is a small company town near the dam. A variety of activities can be enjoyed here. You can tour the **Seattle City Lights Skagit Project**, a mammoth power generating facility. Cruise the waters of the beautiful blue-green Diablo Lake aboard one of two cruise ships. Ride a 53 year old **incline railway** which moves up and down the 560 foot slope of Sourdough Mountain. Or, take in the Upper Skagit River with all its abundant wildlife, beautiful waterfalls, and picturesque snowcapped mountains.

Heading further east you will soon reach Rainy Pass and **Washington Pass**, both provide scenic views not soon forgotten. That's as far east as we go. Only the first section of the Cascade Loop is covered here because it is the primary portion located in the state's northwest corner.

Back at Burlington, if you were to go west rather than east, you would be heading for some of the area's most exciting historical attractions plus the beautiful San Juan Islands. One of the first places you'll want to visit is the town of La Conner.

La Conner got its start in 1868 when Thomas Hayes opened a trading post on the site of what is now Totem Pole Park. Two years later John S. and Louisa A. Conner purchased the post from Hayes and established a post office. Until that time the town had been known as Swinomish. In honor of Louisa it was changed to La Conner.

This is the oldest town in Skagit County and one of the oldest in the state. More than 160 historic buildings and sites can be viewed within the **La Conner Historic District** alone. Most of the downtown area is listed on both the National and State Historic Registers.

To find La Conner head west on Highway 20, out of Burlington, 5 miles to its junction with State 237. Turn left and follow the signs. It's another 5 miles from here and well worth the drive. Besides historic buildings, La Conner also offers a couple of delightful museums, the beautifully restored Gaches Mansion, Indian artifacts, a few nice restaurants, a large marina and public dock plus a variety of shops. It is a very picturesque and quaint, waterfront town. Those who visit in the spring will find the surrounding fields filled with brightly colored tulips, daffodils and irises.

One of the first buildings you'll see upon entering La Conner belongs to the **Tillinghast Seed Company**. Tillinghast was founded in 1885 and first called Puget Sound Seed Gardens. It was originally located at Padilla Station and moved to the present site in 1890. This is the oldest operating store in the Northwest. Inside, besides seeds, you will find posters, signs and seed catalogs dating back as far as 1889, plus antique furnishings, scales and bins from their long ago beginnings. The original printing presses and equipment with which they printed everything necessary for their mail-order seed business, is also on display.

Those interested in viewing the outside of some of La Conner's **older homes** will want to continue west on Morris and turn north on Fourth Street. At the corner of Fourth and Center is the Robert Richardson House. It was constructed in the late 1800's and is one of the more substantial homes built in this area. Richardson was a farmer and owned a livery stable in town. Continue north on Fourth another block and turn left. At the end of this block you will see the old B. L. Martin Home, built in 1893. If you were to take a right turn onto Third Street you would soon arrive at the La Conner Marina.

Heading back to Morris, the house next to the corner of Morris and Second was built in 1892. Directly across Morris is the

Ole Wingren Home, another 1890's building. Ole was a photographer and operated his studio and stationery shop in a small building next door. One block west is the Oak Palace Building. It originally housed the first offices of the Puget Sound Mail newspaper. Next door is another 1890's structure. This was the New Brunswick Hotel and Fair Department Store. The hotel rooms were on top; the department store on the ground floor. Directly across Morris is the historic Magnus Anderson Cabin. It was built in 1869 on Miller's Hill and recently moved to this site. It holds the distinction of being one of the very first structures built in this area.

Turning left on First Street, you'll find lots of historic buildings. You are now in the National Historic District. Second Street too, and parts of Third, are within the district as well. Some of the more outstanding buildings on First include the Lighthouse Inn, 1887 Palace Market, 1896 Town Clothier Building and the Old Fire Hall. The **Firemen's Museum** located here is the permanent home for two 1850 fire wagons. Displayed next to the museum you'll find an 11 foot diameter section of a Douglas fir and a set of wheels used with horse or ox teams in early logging operations.

You can catch a ride on a real **sternwheeler** from the docks in front of the Lighthouse Inn. It will take you on a tour of the Swinomish Channel, out through Hole in the Wall, around Goat Island and back, all aboard the beautifully renovated Emerald Queen paddlewheel boat.

This is also where you will find **Totem Pole Park**, the former site of that 1868 trading post. Today, you can walk where it stood, examine a 24 foot shovel-nose canoe carved by the Swinomish Indians and see a totem pole carved by Lummi Indian Ben Hillaire.

Up the hill, on the corner of Second and Commercial, is a triangular-shaped building that was built in 1886. It originally operated as a bank. Across Commercial, on Second, is the Calhoun House, built in 1878. Calhoun was one of the first physicians to practice in the Pacific Northwest. He also served as the city's first mayor after La Conner's incorporation.

Next door is the **Gaches Mansion**. Tours are available here from May through Labor Day on Fridays, Saturdays and Sundays between 1:00 p.m. and 5:00 p.m. The balance of the year they are only open weekends from 1:00 p.m. to 4:00 p.m. The Gaches Mansion was built in 1891 as a residence. Since that time it has served as a hospital and apartment house as well. In 1974 a group of local citizens bought the fire gutted mansion. Since that time both the exterior and interior have been restored. The fireplaces are original as are the fir floors and cedar woodwork. It has been beautifully furnished befitting its standing. An art museum is located on the second floor and displays works by Northwest artists.

The big white building, across the street, was built in 1875. It was the first Skagit County Courthouse, back when La Conner served as county seat. Two blocks down, on the opposite side of the street behind a grey barn fence, is a house built in 1872 for itinerant Baptist minister B. L. N. Davis.

Down at the bottom of Second Street, in the north end of the La Conner Country Inn, is **Bartlett's World of Antiques**. It is full of coin-operated wonders. Antique music boxes, player pianos and all sorts of musical contraptions are on display. This tiny museum is open Thursday thru Sunday between 10:00 a.m. and 6:00 p.m.

Back up the hill you can visit the **Skagit County Historical Museum**. This is a terrific museum. The people are friendly and the exhibits exciting as well as educational. There are displays on fishing, logging, transportation, mining and Skagit Valley farming activities. A blacksmith shop and a walk-in general store from the early 1900's are there plus Indian and pioneer displays. Between the ornate wood cookstove, peddle powered piano and 1923 Model T Ford, everyone will find their own private treasure.

In the north wing you'll find domestic displays. Early settlers' clothing, their children's toys, books and school gear plus a parlor, bedroom and a full-size, fully equipped farmhouse kitchen. The south wing revolves around how early settlers made their living. That blacksmith shop and walk-in turn of the century general store complete the scene. This is also where you will find the Northwest Coastal Indian display. The east wing is used for special exhibits and display of historic photographs. It also offers a panoramic view of the surrounding area.

The museum is open year round, Wednesday thru Sunday, from 1:00 p.m. to 5:00 p.m.

Heading south of town, turn on Maple and head across Rainbow Bridge. This road leads to the Reservation belonging to the Swinomish Tribe. Just before you reach the Shelter Bay road you will encounter the **Swinomish Indian Cemetery**, one of the oldest in the state. It's particularly colorful around Memorial Day when the Swinomish decorate the graves in a traditional ceremony. Continuing along Reservation Road you will also find **St. Paul's Catholic Church**. This church was built in 1868 and was part of the Mission Trail from California. It has been extensively renovated.

Back on Highway 20, if you were to turn right onto Highway 237 you would soon arrive at the **Padilla Bay National Estuarine Sanctuary**. It is one of only eight national estuaries and protects the largest undisturbed tideflat area in Puget Sound. It includes 11,600 acres with 8 miles of nature trails, wildlife habitat areas and controlled public tideland access.

More than 237 different species of birds have been identified in the Padilla Bay area. An average of 50,000 ducks alone winter here each year. Large flocks of American wigeon, mallard, pintail, greenwinged teal, northern shoveler and sandpipers are common.

As many as 57 species of fish have been identified in the bay's water and 14 different mammals along its shores. Black-tailed deer, harbor seal, river otter, raccoon, red fox, coyote, muskrat and beaver are included. Sometimes as many as 70 harbor seals have been observed using the sandy-mud flats and tidal channels in the southern part of Padilla Bay.

At the **Breazeale-Padilla Bay Interpretive Center** you will find hands on exhibits, guided nature walks, films and a wealth of knowledge about marine biology and the environment of Padilla Bay.

Returning to Highway 20 it's another 11 miles to **Anacortes**, situated on the northwestern shores of Fidalgo Island. The island is formed by Padilla Bay and the Swinomish Channel which separate it from the rest of Skagit County. Prior to the establishment of the Swinomish Indian Reservation in 1873 it was a favored hunting and fishing spot for local tribesmen.

Fishing is still very popular here. At Lake Campbell, 3 miles south of town, you'll find bass, catfish, perch, rainbow trout and spineyray. This 410 acre lake has a launching ramp and is a favorite with water-skiers as well as fishermen. Little Cranberry Lake, just west of town, is loaded with bass, perch and spineyrays. No motors are allowed on the lake. Lake Erie, 2 miles south of town, has a public boat ramp and lots of rainbow trout. Pass Lake is found in Deception Pass State Park and offers fly fishermen a chance at rainbow and cutthroat trout. No motorboats are allowed on the lake.

Non-Indian settlers first made their appearance here in 1853. In 1879 Amos Bowman established the area's first post office designating it the "Anna Curtis Post Office", for his wife Anna Curtis Bowman. The name was later adapted to Anacortes. Bowman was convinced Anacortes would prosper as the western terminus for the Canadian Pacific Railroad. When they declined he negotiated with one railroad after another, attempting to bring a transcontinental rail terminus to Anacortes. By 1890 there were five rival railroad depots built in the town and land had soared from $2 an acre to $500 and more. Town now included 47 saloons, 27 real estate offices, 12 hotels, 8 tobacco stores, 7 churches, 4 grocery stores, 3 shoe stores, 2 drug stores, 2 banks, 2 newspapers and a school. In 1893 that boom came to a sudden halt and Anacortes dried up into a near-ghost town. Today the population is over 9,000 and visitors come from world-wide to enjoy its beauty.

The **Anacortes Museum**, at 8th and M Avenue, is housed in the former Carnegie Library building. The main exhibit area includes a collection of Northwest Indian artifacts, a turn of the century parlor, and numerous items related to early community activities and industry. A reconstructed cannery office is also on display. Materials used here were salvaged from one of the area's earliest salmon canneries; it was in operation from the 1890's to 1925. Office shelves hold the original cannery records. In the lower gallery you will find special exhibits and programs.

The fountain out front was given to the city by the Women's Temperance Union and was originally located in the business district. It sports drinking basins at varying heights for dogs, cats, horses and men. It is not known whether or not the drinking fountain had much effect on saloon business. The museum is open Wednesday thru Sunday between 1:00 p.m. and 4:30 p.m. They are closed on all major holidays.

The **Washington Ferry System** stops in Anacortes. From here they make daily trips to the Canadian city of Sydney. Ports-of-call in the San Juans include San Juan, Lopez, Shaw and Orcas Islands. These islands are discussed in detail in the San Juan portion of this book. The ferry terminal is located at Ship Harbor, on the west end of Anacortes. It is reached by driving west on 12th Street from the city center.

Skagit County operates a small ferry between Anacortes and Guemes Island. This ferry terminal is located at 6th and I Avenue. It takes only 10 minutes for the ferry to reach the landing on the south shore of Guemes Island.

The W. T. Preston is a **historic sternwheeler** that sits dry-docked just north of the Cap Sante Boat Haven, at 7th and R Avenue. This 161 foot stern paddle boat is listed on the National Register of Historic Places. It first went into service in 1914 with the U. S. Army Engineers. The steel hull was added in 1939.

Totem poles can be seen at Island View Public School near 26th and J Avenue, Washington Park, and 9th and E Avenue. All are recent carvings.

Mt. Erie, near the center of the island via Heart Lake Road, is a terrific place to survey the surrounding land. From its 1,270 foot summit you can see the Selkirk Mountains to the north, Mt. Baker and the Cascade Mountains to the northeast, Mount Rainier to the southeast, the Olympic Mountains to the southwest, and the San Juan Archipelago and Vancouver Island to the west. The bronze and stone sculpture at the mountain's top was placed there in memory of the man who donated this land to the city of Anacortes and the public, as a wildlife sanctuary.

In all, Anacortes has nearly a dozen beautiful parks. **Washington Park** is another one that offers some very scenic views. From here you can see much of Puget Sound. Most of the park's 3 mile loop road winds through thickly forested, rocky hillsides that look down over the beaches of Burrows Bay. Hiking trails, campsites, a boat launch and picnic facilities are all available. To find the park, take 12th out of the city center, this soon becomes Oakes Avenue. When the road heads right, toward the ferry harbor, follow Sunset Avenue left toward Green Point and the park.

Fidalgo Island is joined to Whidbey Island at **Deception Pass**. They are connected by a picturesque 200 foot high bridge that spans the 1,350 foot wide split. It too offers a spectacular view. This is also the site of the 2,500 acre Deception Pass State Park. Lands within the park's boundaries lie at both ends of the bridge. An environmental learning center, 4 miles of sandy beaches, hiking trails leading through majestic stands of virgin timber, both fresh and salt water swimming, picnic tables and lots of great viewpoints make it a good place to stop.

Whidbey is the second longest island in the continental United States. It was thought by early Spanish explorers to be a part of the mainland. This pass, separating the two islands, was discovered in 1792 by Joseph Whidbey under the command of Captain George Vancouver.

This is part of the **San Juan Islands**; 172 individual island paradises. Most of these islands are accessible only by private boat; a few receive regular ferry service. Some of the smaller islands are covered entirely by state parks; others by wildlife refuges. All reflect lushly against the sparkling blue waters. Many reminders of the area's still visible history are protected here offering visitors a terrific opportunity to explore the past.

Just a short distance south of the Deception Pass Bridge you will find a junction for Coronet Bay Road. This road leads to Hoypus Point. The **Coronet Bay Heron Rookery** is about half way to the point. This is a protected refuge; you should not disturb these birds in any way. During late winter and early spring months you will often see bald eagles around Hoypus Point.

Return to the main road and continue heading south. Soon you will come to **Fort Ebey State Park**. It too offers campsites, picnic tables, a fishing lake, excellent hiking trails, and outstanding views.

Fort Ebey is one of two former Whidbey Island U.S. Army forts that have been turned into state parks. This fort was built in 1942 as part of the World War II defensive build-up. It provided two 6-inch guns designed for use against ships attempting to enter Puget Sound. Today its hiking trails provide access to the lush forest environment of its surroundings leading you to a number of places from which to watch for birds, whales, ships and submarines entering and leaving the Sound.

The Point Partridge Beach area is known for its "kettles". These were created during the retreat of the last glaciers when blocks of buried ice were left behind causing these interesting depressions in the earth.

You can also visit the **Ebey's Landing National Historic Reserve**. This reserve protects a rural community that is teeming with historic sights; and provides an unbroken record of the days when Puget Sound was first explored and settled, to the present time. As a national historic reserve, it commemorates the explorations of Captain George Vancouver in 1792, the settlement of Whidbey Island prior to 1850 by Colonel Issac Neff Ebey, early island settlers and homesteaders. Fort Ebey State Park, Grasser's Hill and Lagoon, Monroe's Landing, the town of Coupeville, Ebey's Landing, Fort Casey State Park, Crockett Lake and Uplands, and Smith Prairie are all included within the reserve's boundaries.

Grasser's Hill and Lagoon was the site of a land claim filed in 1852. It is just northeast of Fort Ebey State Park. Monroe's Landing is just a bit farther east via Penn Cove Road. It was explored in 1792 by Joseph Whidbey. Their journals show that they were met *"by upwards of two hundred Indians, some in canoes with their families, and other walking along the shore attended by about forty dogs in a drove, shorn close to the skin like sheep."* The dogs mentioned here were found only in the Northwest. They were said to be about the size of a fox and kept by the Indians for their hair, which was mixed with plant fibers and feathers and woven into blankets.

The streets of **Coupeville** are lined with authentic false-front buildings and hundred year old homes. There's Alexander's Blockhouse built in 1855, the 1852 Fairhaven log cabin, 1874 Masonic Hall, 1894 Methodist Church and the 1889 First Congregational Church, plus another two dozen homes built between 1854 and 1899. This whole town is listed on the National Register of Historic Places. Two good places to start your tour are the informative National Park exhibit on Front, or the **Island County Historical Museum**. You can get a self-guided tour sheet at the museum for a minimal charge.

This museum is located in a former firehall. Permanent displays include Indian baskets, dolls, furnishings from the 1891 Island County Courthouse, area momentos and a Wurlitzer Military Band Organ complete with drum, cymbal and horns. Changing exhibits are also brought in from time to time. In addition to the museum proper, there is a display on Coveland Street which contains a 1902 Holsman Auto Buggy. Museum hours are weekends only during April and May and Wednesdays thru Sundays from June thru September between 1:00 p.m. and 5:00 p.m.

Ebey's Landing can be easily reached by taking Ebey Road a short distance across the island. This is also the site of the now unused 1860 Ferry House. The cabins located a few yards south of the Ferry House is Isaac N. Ebey's original home. Ebey led the first permanent white settlers to Whidbey Island after his own 1850 arrival. It was because of this leadership that area Indians considered him to be head man. In August of 1857 they shot and beheaded Ebey in retaliation for the killing of their own chief near Port Gamble in October of the prior year. Ebey is buried on the hill north of his claim, in Sunnyside Cemetery, along with other early pioneers. The cemetery is also the site of the James C. Davis Blockhouse.

Fort Casey State Park too was once a U.S. Army fort. It was built during the late 1890's. By 1908 Fort Casey had become the fourth largest military post in the state. Near the end of World War II, when airplanes became capable of accurate aerial bombings, the guns from Fort Casey were melted down. In 1956 the property was transferred to the Washington State Parks Department. Since then, two old guns with the 1900 vintage retractable carriages were found and mounted at Fort Casey as an exhibit from a bygone time. The Admiralty Head Lighthouse, which was erected in 1860 and rebuilt in 1902, is also a rehabilitated exhibit.

This state park offers a lovely underwater reserve for scuba divers plus picnic sites, surf fishing and hiking trails.

The **Washington Ferry System** operates between Fort Casey and beautifully historic Port Townsend on the Olympic Peninsula. For information on what to see in Port Townsend, refer to the Upper Olympic Peninsula section of this book. Another ferry runs between Clinton, at the southern end of Whidbey Island, and Mukilteo, on the mainland. To visit other islands in the San Juan Archipelago you must either travel by private boat or take the ferry out of Anacortes. It makes stops on San Juan, Lopez, Shaw, and Orcas Islands.

Forty-five minutes out of Anacortes the ferry makes its first stop at **Lopez Island**. This island is mostly agricultural with its small orchards, grazing cattle and pastureland interspersed with green forests. Because Lopez Island is relatively flat, once you get past the ferry landing hill, it is a favorite spot for bicyclists.

Odlin County Park is found 1.3 miles south of the ferry landing. It covers 80 acres and offers 30 campsites, stoves, water and toilets. Explorers will find its wooded landscape peaceful and inviting. **Agate Beach County Park**, on the southern tip of the island, offers no overnight camping but serves as a terrific place for a picnic. It is also a good place to watch for sea life and explore tide pools; as is nearby Iceberg Point.

Spencer Spit State Park is located on the northeast side of the island. This land was originally homesteaded in the 1850's. Today the pristine beauty of its wooded lands, and the driftwood scattered sandy spit, is a public park. Picnic facilities are available as well as 45 campsites plus fishing, clamming, beachwalking and swimming.

Hummel Lake, just a few miles east of Lopez Village, is a popular spot with fishermen. Bluegill, catfish and rainbow trout can all be caught here. No motors are allowed on the lake.

Shaw Island is the ferry's second stop after leaving Anacortes. Since this island is not set up for tourists, most people visit Shaw Island only by day. **Indian Cove**, two miles from the ferry landing, offers a sandy beach perfect for an all day picnic. Hikers and bicyclists will also enjoy the island's 11 miles of quiet public roads. The three acre island found off the bay is Blind Island. It is one of the state's many marine parks located in these waters.

It's only a 10 minute ferry ride from Shaw to **Orcas Island**, the largest of all the San Juan Islands. Orcas features some of the most spectacular terrain of all the islands. It includes over 125 miles of salt water coastline, innumerable coves, bays, harbors and sounds.

You'll find public access to all this beauty across the island, at the 5,000 acre **Moran State Park**. It is difficult to match the 360 degree panoramic view you'll get from the summit of Moran's Mt. Constitution. Bicyclists will enjoy the park's 30 miles of biking trails. Hikers too will find it exceptional. Some of the more popular hikes are the steep 1.5 mile trail from the top of Mt. Constitution to Twin Lakes and the 2.5 mile path between Twin and Mountain Lakes. This park also includes some beautiful waterfalls.

The **Orcas Island Historical Museum** is located near the heart of Eastsound. This is where you will find the world famous Ethan Allen collection of Indian artifacts, plus many beautiful early pioneer furnishings and heirlooms. The building is made up of the former pioneer cabins of six early Island families. The museum is open from the July 4th weekend until Labor Day weekend, Monday thru Saturday, from 1:00 p.m. to 4:00 p.m. At other times of the year you must call 376-4667 for an appointment.

Orcas Island is also the site of Washington State's largest resort. The Rosario Resort was expanded from the 1905, 54-room **Moran Mansion**. This mansion was built to last. The foundation was chiseled from solid rock. Next came three stories built of solid concrete and topped with a roof containing six tons of sheet copper. The music room on the second floor is equipped with an Aeolian pipe organ. Organ concerts and historical tours of the mansion are offered Wednesdays through Sundays. You must call the resort for specific times, 376-2222.

Orcas Island Pottery, just southwest of Eastsound, has a log cabin sales room that is over 100 years old. The main building houses a storeroom, workroom and living quarters. Visitors are welcome to watch the potters work thru the workroom windows.

Friday Harbor, on **San Juan Island**, is the last U.S. stop for the Washington Ferry. This town is the county seat and offers two museums; one for history buffs and one for those interested in whales.

The **Whale Museum** is located on First Street, across from the post office. Displays range from an entire orca skelton to a fossilized dolphin brain. The museum tells of whale evolution, species identification, migrations, feeding methods, social behavior, and more. There is a Childrens' Room as well as a library and video viewing room.

In the upper reaches of Puget Sound, approximately 80 Orca whales live year round in three family groups, or pods. Other area inhabitants include 17 minke whales, occasional gray whales, and an undetermined number of Dalls and harbor porpoises. The Whale Museum is a project of the Moclips Cetological Society and offers classes which include whale viewing.

The **San Juan Historical Museum** is found in the old James King farm homestead, just outside Friday Harbor. The house was constructed around the turn of the century and is packed with period furnishings and pioneer memorabilia. A 1917 Cadillac fire truck and the town's original 1892 jail are also part of this display. The museum is open from Memorial Day to Labor Day on Wednesdays and Saturdays only between 1:00 p.m. and 4:00 p.m. For off season tours call 378-4587.

About 1 mile from the ferry landing you will spot a turnoff to the University of Washington **Marine Field Laboratories**. Guided tours are given during July and August between 2:00 p.m. and 4:00 p.m., on Wednesdays and Saturdays. The grounds and outside tank can be viewed at any time.

Two national parks can be found on this island as well. Both provide a look at the remaining reminders of the 1859-1872 English/American Pig War. At the 529 acre **English Camp National Historic Park** you can see three of the original buildings. A lovely woodland hike leads uphill from English Camp to the English Cemetery. This war, although begun over an English owned pig shot by a renegade American, was actually about the settlement of the boundary between the United States and Great Britain. The Oregon Treaty of 1846 had settled part of the international boundary question, but a conflict persisted, concerning the water boundary between Vancouver Island and what is now the state of Washington.

The 1200 acre **American Camp National Historic Park** is located at the southern end of San Juan Island. In 1860, after 100 men from the British Light Infantry set up the English

Camp, 100 American soldiers raised the U.S. flag here on the opposite side of the island. They then built barracks and remained as a garrison. Historic points of interest are well marked along the trails. Both parks are limited to day use, and allow public access to miles of beach area. Both Cattle Point and Eagle Cove provide excellent opportunities to observe sea life at low tide.

San Juan County Park is found on the island's west side and covers 12 acres. Campsites are at a premium here, with only 18 spots available. This is a very popular place with scuba divers. The bay seems to intrigue beginning divers while the more experienced head for the waters along the rocky bluffs. More campsites can be found at Lakedale, midway between Friday and Roche Harbors.

If you follow the three-mile section of gravel road, just past the county park, you will soon descend a steep hill to find an outstanding view. This sweeping panorama includes the Olympic Mountains, Vancouver Island, and the Strait of Juan de Fuca. The side road, off to the right, leads to **Limekiln Lighthouse**. Past the gate, on your left, is a trail to some bluffs above a rocky shoreline where waves crash at your feet and ships pass by in the distance.

The rest of the islands do not have ferry service and are accessible only by private boat. On the north end of **Cypress Island** you'll find public mooring buoys, trails, picnic facilities and 5 campsites. On the west side, in Strawberry Bay, the Strawberry Island Marine Park provides more picnic sites.

Hope Island is a state marine park. Mooring buoys can be found along the north shore; a sandy beach on the south shore. **James Island** is another state marine park. The entire 113 acre island is included and offers a dock, mooring buoys, campsites, picnic tables and trails. Hiking, fishing, swimming, clamming and scuba diving are all popular here.

Patos Island is the northernmost of all the San Juan Islands and holds a 200 acre state park. **Saddlebag Island** consists of 23 acres which are entirely covered by a marine park. There is a bay on the north side and another on the south. Picnic sites and trails are on shore.

Sinclair Island, just northwest of Guemes Island, has a 35 acre natural area preserved by the Washington Department of Game. A variety of song birds frequent this area during the summer and various raptors and waterfowl may be seen throughout the fall and winter months.

Skagit Island was the turn-of-the-century hideout for a smuggler known as The Flying Dutchman. Today the Skagit Island Marine Park covers the entire island. State park buoys are located off the northwest shore of the island and a few campsites can be found on shore. Watch your approach, the water between Skagit and Kiket Islands is treacherous for boats.

Three state parks can be found on **Stuart Island**. Reid, Prevost Harbor and Turn Point are all accessible by boat. The **Sucia Islands** consist of nearly a dozen tiny islands with a combined total of 562 acres. They are all part of one large state park. These beaches are great for treasure hunting and picnics. Lovely time sculpted sandstone rocks and caves dot the shore. This is another area that is very popular with scuba divers.

The **San Juan Islands Wildlife Refuge** consists of 84 islands totaling 458 acres. Close-up wildlife observation is permitted only on Matia, Turn and Jones Island. The balance of the refuge is set aside primarily for the protection of its large variety of birds. Gulls, cormorants, scooters, guillemots, puffins, auklets, oystercatchers and shorebirds all nest here. Many of the refuge's islands appear to be nothing more than protruding rocks and unnamed islets.

Jones Island is just off the southwest shore of Orcas Island. All of its 188 acres are a state park featuring beachcombing, fishing, hiking and skin diving. As with nearly all of the smaller islands, you'll need to bring your own fresh water. A few campsites, picnic tables and fireplaces can be found on the island.

Matia Island is just north of Orcas Island and provides a dock, mooring buoys, picnic tables and water. The island has a 150 acre wildlife refuge plus a 5 acre park that offers boaters a spot to touch ground. This is another spot where fishing, hiking and scuba diving are popular.

Turn Island is jointly managed by Washington State and the U.S. Forest and Wildlife Service. It is open to the public as a marine park. You'll find great tide pools here but no fresh water.

Heading south out of Burlington, you'll find **Mount Vernon** is just a five minute drive. This town was established in 1870 and named after George Washington's estate on the Potomac River. **Hillcrest Park**, at 11th and Fowler, is located in a forest-type setting and offers a mini-zoo, Oriental garden, sheltered picnic areas, playground equipment, modern restrooms, and 4 lighted tennis courts. The mini-zoo is only open between 9:00 a.m. and 4:00 p.m., weekdays, from June 1st through September 1st.

At **Little Mountain City Park** you can stretch your legs on one of the fine hiking trails or check out the observation tower, which offers a view of Skagit Valley and Puget Sound. This 490 acre park is reached by following Blackburn Road to Little Mountain Road. Edgewater Park, west of town along the Skagit River, provides campsites and fishing. The Skagit River is famous for steelhead trout fishing.

At the **Washington Cheese Company** viewing windows allow you to see how cheese is made. Afterwards, you can sample the product. Over 30,000 pounds of cheese are produced here each day. They are open daily from 9:00 a.m. to 5:30 p.m. but closed on Sundays. Off I-5 you would take the College Way Exit (#227) to 900 East College Way.

Southwest of **Conway** white pelicans, sandhill cranes, pigeon hawks and nearly 200 other species of birds have been sighted. At the **Skagit Wildlife Recreation Area** good viewing spots include the Big Ditch Slough, where you'll usually find plenty of wood ducks, and Barney Lake, which is noted for its trumpeter swans.

Continuing south on I-5, Highway 530 is the exit to **Darrington** and will prove to be particularly exciting to folks who enjoy outdoor activities. Your first stop should be the local forest service office where you can get individual guidance and information about **Glacier Peak Wilderness**. This 464,219 acre protected wilderness includes 350 miles of maintained trails. These range from easy hikes to strenuous mountain scaling. This is an area of heavy forests, steep valleys and dramatic glacier peaks.

During the winter, many of Darrington's back roads provide a haven for snowmobilers. Crevice Creek, Segelson Pass and Goodman Creek Roads are all good routes. Check with the folks at the Darrington forest service office for details on these and other established snowmobile trails. Cross-country skiers will find French Creek Road (#2010), Prairie Mountain Road (#2140), Round Mountain Road (#1890) and Suiattle River Road (#26) all great.

Heading south again on I-5, **Marysville** will soon come into view. Founded in 1872, its earliest beginnings were derived from trade with the Tulalip Indians. **Totem poles** can be viewed at Comeford Park, the Veteran's Hall and the entrance to the Tulalip Tribal Center. They were all carved by local Indians many years ago.

If you go west on Marine Drive about 13 miles, you'll arrive at **Kayak Point Park**. This 670 acre park offers a day use beach area with 3300 feet of shoreline. Facilities include picnic tables, fire pits, restrooms, a boat launch and a 300 foot fishing pier. An overnight camping area is open during the summer season, on the bluff above the beach.

Everett is 5 miles south of Marysville. This is where the Cascade Loop makes its return and the Mukilteo Ferry deposits and picks up its Whidbey Island passengers. Public access to the **waterfront** is available at Marine View Drive and 21st Street. Huge ships from foreign ports, waterfront workers, the Mukilteo Ferry, log booms, fish packing operations, fishermen and pleasure boaters can all be seen along the water. This is a working waterfront, so be sure to stay alert and keep clear of loading and unloading areas.

Rucker Hill had its beginnings when the town relied heavily on logging as its main industry. During the late 1800's, this is where the local lumber barons all built their stately homes. Rucker Avenue, between 10th and 20th Streets, has changed little since that time. In fact, Rucker Hill has been designated as a historical district.

The Everett Parks and Recreation Department maintains 25 local parks. Most of their small neighborhood and community parks offer picnic facilities, playground equipment and a place to stretch your legs. South of Rucker Hill you can visit **Forest Park**, covering 111 acres and offering hiking trails, game areas, picnic facilities, an animal farm and wading pool. The animal farm offers hands-on experience with barnyard animals, but is open only during the summer.

At Everett's 142 acre American Legion Memorial Park, on the north end of town, you'll find all of the usual amenities plus an arboretum and a historical museum. The **Snohomish County Historical Museum** is only open on Sundays between 2:00 p.m. and 6:00 p.m.

If you enjoy airplanes, and would like a tour of a **Boeing 747/767 Assembly Plant**, Everett is the place to go. Their main factory is said to be the most modern aircraft manufacturing facility of its kind. Eight 747's and eight 767's can be in final assembly here, all at the same time. The building towers 11 stories upward and covers 62 acres. The tour begins with a film, then heads to an observation perch where you view a host of planes in various stages of assembly, as workers rivet and install the several million pieces that make up each plane.

Tours are given weekdays at 9:00 a.m. and 12:30 p.m. Children under 12 are not admitted. The plant is located at 3303 Casino Road South.

South of Everett 6 miles, is **Snohomish**, a town begun in the 1850's. The original settlement centered around the present-day library building between Cedar and Maple. As you tour this town you'll find that many of the elegant homes built by early residents and lumber barons remain intact.

The **Blackman Museum** is in one of those old homes. It was built in 1878 by a prominent local lumberman as a place upon which he could display the shingles made at his mill. The owner, Hyrcanus Blackman, was also Snohomish's first mayor. His home has been restored and furnished with period antiques and is open to the public on weekends, between noon and 4:00 p.m. You will find this museum at 118 Avenue B.

The folks at the museum can also supply you with a **historic home tour** map that will guide you past 25 other historical buildings. Avenues A, B, C and D, between 1st and 5th, all sport elegant, old homes and buildings. This town's nickname is the *"antique capital of the northwest"*. More than 90 antique dealers are said to do business within an easily walked 4 block area of downtown Snohomish.

You can also view an authentic totem pole at Kla Ha Ya Park. Another park, found where Marshland Road intersects with Highway 9, contains a **"bicycle tree"**. This is an ancient tall cedar measuring 48 feet around. Turn of the century bicyclists paid a logger $15 to carve an archway allowing their path to pass right through its trunk.

You'll find **Flowing Lake Park** east of town. This 42 acre lakefront park has a day use area with a swimming beach, picnic facilities, playground equipment, restrooms, campsites and a boat launch. A nature trail has been blazed through the wooded portion of the park. To reach the park, follow Highway 2 two miles and turn left on 99th Street. Just past the French Creek Grange, bear left on 171st Avenue. Turn right on 48th Street and follow it to the park.

Flowing Lake is said to offer some decent **fishing**. Other area fishing lakes include Storm and Panther. Rainbow trout, perch and cutthroats can be found at Blackman Lake. Local fishermen rate this one of their best close-in spots. The Snohomish River has a summer steelhead season, and you can fish the Pilchuck River in the winter.

The **Pilchuck River** is also a great place for summer innertubing. You can start as far upriver as time allows, and float an hour or all day. The ride ends at Pilchuck Park where the Pilchuck River joins Snohomish River.

Museum lovers will want to visit **Edmonds**, which is southwest of Snohomish. At 118 Fifth Avenue North, you'll find a brick and stone building which is listed on the National Register of Historic Buildings. Inside the **Edmonds Museum** is a collection of nineteenth century furniture and household furnishings, early day carpenter, shipping and logging tools, axes and saws, a working model of a turn of the century shingle mill, maritime memorabilia and photographs. The museum is open Tuesdays, Thursdays and Sundays only, from 1:00 p.m. to 4:00 p.m.

Seattle is the most southerly point to be included in this book. It was the site of the world's fair in 1962. The **Space Needle** is just one of the fascinating reminders you'll find of its excitement. You can take an elevator to the top of this 605 foot structure for an unmatchable revolving view. It is open seven days a week.

The **Seattle Center** is a 74 acre area of beautifully landscaped grounds, surrounding the Space Needle. This urban park is always bustling with activity. An opera house, playhouse, coliseum, sports arena, museums, amusement park, crafts center, science center and more can all be found at this one location. Walk around the grounds and visit the International Fountain, or one of thirteen other artistic fountains that dot the grounds. The Center House offers a variety of family entertainment year round, and the outdoor amphitheater is a favorite spot for summertime concerts. The Horiuchi mosaic mural that serves as a backdrop for the amphitheater is worth a stop, even if there is no concert going on.

The **Pacific Science Center** houses over 120 "hands-on" exhibits plus a children's area and a Laserium, offering sound and light shows. While there you can take part in computer games, mazes and mathematical puzzles. They are open daily, 10:00 a.m. to 5:00 p.m., weekends they stay open until 6:00 p.m.

Another reminder of that past world's fair is the **Monorail**. In just 90 seconds flat, it will transport you from the Seattle Center to downtown Seattle's Westlake Mall. The ride is a real treat and it does away with all those worries about where to park.

Antique trolleys have gone back to work along the Elliott Bay waterfront. Originally built in 1927, these ingeniously fashioned cars were recently rescued from early retirement in Melbourne, Australia. They leave the barn across from Pier 70 to make their way along the waterfront accompanied by the nostalgic sounds of trolley whistles and bells. Hours of operation are 6:00 a.m. to 6:00 p.m.

At 704 Terry, visit the **Charles & Emma Frye Art Museum**. The Fryes came to Seattle in 1888 and lived a short distance from the museum that today houses their extensive private art collection. Their wills left 230 paintings and the funding necessary to build and operate a public art museum. In addition to this permanent collection there are contemporary art exhibits as well. The hours are 10:00 a.m. to 5:00 p.m. Monday thru Saturday and noon to 5:00 p.m. Sundays.

The **Seattle Art Museum** is at Prospect and 14th Street East. They are open Tuesday thru Saturday from 10:00 a.m. to 5:00 p.m., Sundays from noon till 5:00 p.m., and offer evening viewing on Thursdays until 9:00 p.m. Outstanding permanent displays include contemporary 20th century paintings and sculpture, Renaissance and European paintings and sculpture, Asian art, and a decorative arts collection plus continual changing exhibits of photography, paintings, sculpture and graphics. This museum also coordinates the modern art pavilion at Seattle Center which sees exhibit changes about six times a year.

The **Seattle Conservatory** is made up of five separate, though linked, greenhouses and is located at nearby Volunteer Park. Each houses a different collection. In the center, Palm House offers large tropical plants and an extraordinary orchid collection. Ferns, seasonal floral displays, bromeliads and cacti fill the others. Summer hours are 10:00 a.m. to 7:00 p.m. They close at 4:00 p.m. the balance of the year.

Between Main and Weller Streets, 5th and 8th Avenues, you'll find Seattle's International District, commonly referred to as **China Town**. This area is home to many Chinese, Japanese, Filipino and Javanese Americans. It's loaded with colorful grocery stores, restaurants and small shops reflecting their cultures. Hing Hay Park features a colorful Chinese pavilion and is often the site of Chinese folk dances, martial arts exhibits and other events from the Far East. The Nippon Kan Theatre is a National Historic Site and the start of a China Town tour.

A trip to Seattle's International District is incomplete without a stop at the **Wing Luke Memorial Museum**, 414 8th Avenue South. You'll find cultural exhibits, Asian folk art, Chinese fans, photographs and parasols all on display. The museum is open Tuesday thru Friday from 11:00 a.m. to 4:30 p.m. and Saturdays from noon to 4:00 p.m.

You can also get a tour at **Pioneer Square**, this one takes you underground, into Seattle's colorful past. Reservations are recommended, 682-4646. It was here that the first sawmills, port facilities and businesses grew only to be consumed in the great fire of 1889. Most of the buildings in the Pioneer Square Historic District date from between 1889 and 1900.

You can take your own tour, without the underground portion, by starting at the triangle park at First and Yesler. This has been a popular meeting place since before the turn of the century. If you simply head south on First for four blocks, you will see several stone and brick buildings. There is the 1897 Mutual Life Building, 1890 Yesler Building, 1900 Lippy Building, 1895 Terry-Denny Building, 1890 Maynard Building, 1895 Selmar Building, 1889 Grand Central Hotel, 1889 New England Building, 1898 Globe Building and many others.

The **Klondike Gold Rush National Historic Park** protects that area too. It was here, along these Seattle streets, that prospectors bought their supplies, boarded ships and headed north to Alaska in search of gold. The National Park Department maintains an information center at 117 S. Main Street. They are open most days from 9:00 a.m. to 5:00 p.m. and can provide you with maps and information about the rich heritage of both the gold rush days and Pioneer Square Historic District.

You can visit the **Alki Point Light Station** on weekends and holidays between 1:00 p.m. and 4:00 p.m. Coast Guard personnel are there to answer your questions and let you look around inside. The light station is located at 3201 Alki Avenue SW and is over 100 years old.

The **West Point Lighthouse** is at the western end of Discovery Park. Coast Guard personnel welcome visitors here on weekends and holidays, between 1:00 p.m. and 5:00 p.m.

The **U.S. Coast Guard's Northwest Museum** is located at 1519 Alaskan Way South. It houses a collection that includes 2500 artifacts, 9000 photos, a number of beautiful ship models plus over 2000 articles, clippings, books and miscellaneous items relating to the Coast Guard's early history in the Pacific Northwest and Alaska. The museum is open most afternoons, except Thursdays, and on weekends between 1:00 p.m. and 5:00 p.m. Pier 36 is also the home of two large Polar icebreakers, and two high endurance cutters. The cutters are open to visitors on Saturday and Sunday afternoons.

Visit the **Western Union Museum** and learn all about the early beginnings of this important form of communication. You'll be able to see early equipment and learn about the part it played in our lives. The museum is at 312 Occidental South. It is open Monday thru Friday from 8:30 a.m. to 8:00 p.m., Saturdays from 9:00 a.m. to 7:00 p.m., and Sundays from 9:00 a.m. until 4:00 p.m.

You can see exhibits covering anthropology, geology and zoology at the University of Washington's **Thomas Burke Memorial Museum**. Established in 1885, this is the oldest university museum still in operation in the West. Museum hours are 11:00 a.m. to 5:30 p.m., Tuesday thru Friday, and 9:00 a.m. to 4:30 p.m., Saturday and Sunday.

The Observatory across Memorial Way was built in 1895. The telescope was manufactured in 1891. Both are still in use and offer free viewing. Call 543-2888 for a schedule.

The University of Washington has a 346 acre campus and is open to the public year round. Explore, picnic, study the architecture, feed the squirrels, sit and watch the fountains, read the plaques and marvel at the statues. Campus maps and information on campus events are available at the Visitors Information Center. The office is closed on all school holidays.

The **Woodland Park Zoo** contains exotic birds, beasts, and reptiles, as well as a popular children's zoo and Nocturnal House. You will find it just west of Green Lake at 50th and Fremont Avenue North. They're particularly proud of their African Savanna and Gorilla Exhibits. They are open seven days a week from 8:30 a.m. to 4:00 p.m. with extended hours, till 6:00 p.m., from April through September.

Ye Olde Curiosity Shop first opened in 1899. It contains some rare collectors items and some real odd curiosities. For instance, there's Sylvester, a 6 foot mummy found in the Gila Bend Desert in 1895. Sylvester is perfectly preserved and weighs 137 pounds. For company, he is joined by a collection of shrunken heads. This is said to be the largest collection in existence outside Ecuador, and includes a shrunken torso and the world's smallest adult shrunken head.

On the lighter side you'll find exquisitely hand tooled elephant and walrus ivory, finely carved totem poles, handmade Eskimo soapstone carvings, an extensive antique weapons collection and thousands of other items. This is perhaps, as the folks there like to claim, the most unique shop in the world. They are located at 601 Alaskan Way.

The Upper Olympic Peninsula

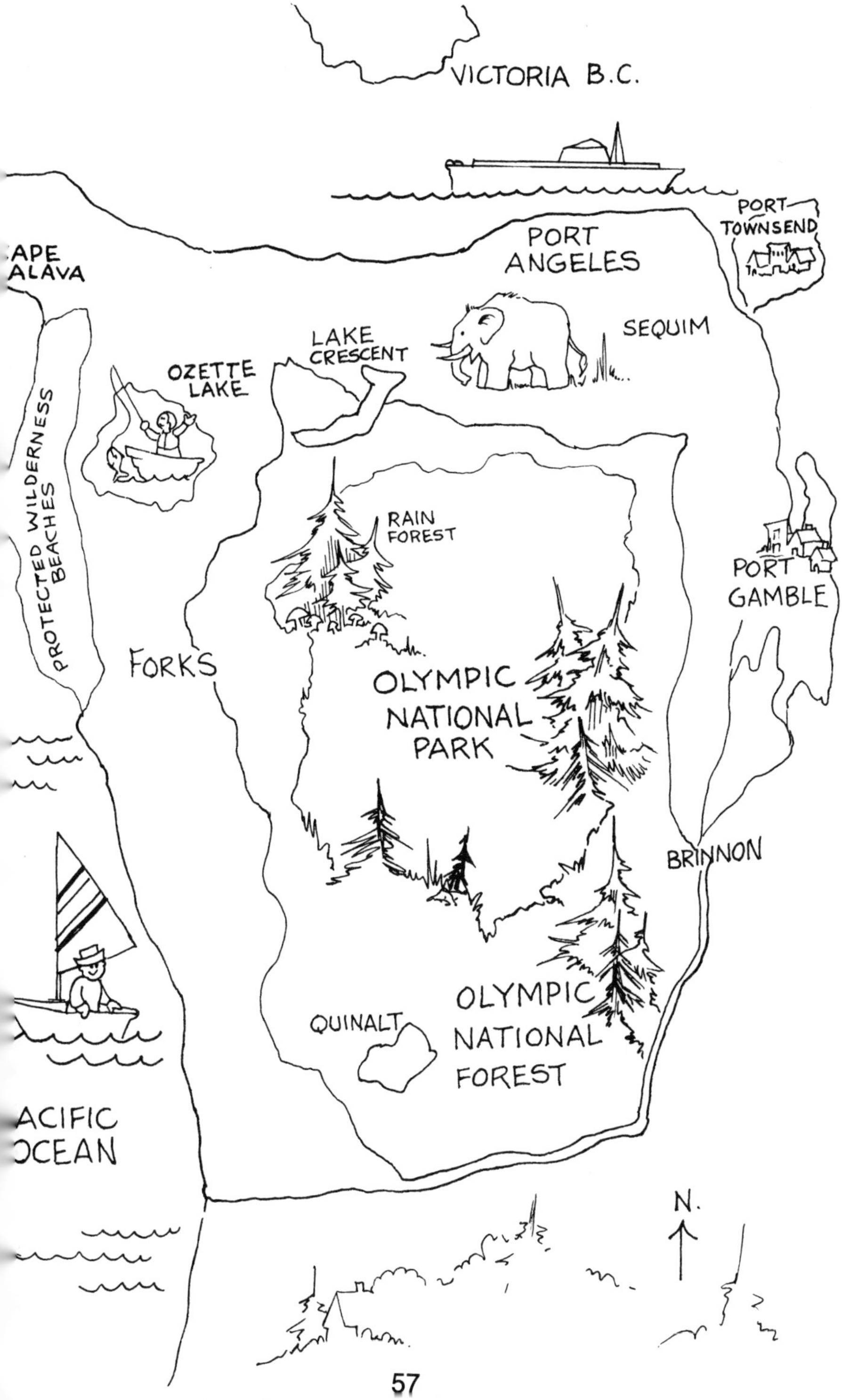

VICTORIA B.C.

PORT
TOWNSEND

PORT
ANGELES

CAPE
ALAVA

SEQUIM

LAKE
CRESCENT

OZETTE
LAKE

PROTECTED WILDERNESS
BEACHES

RAIN
FOREST

PORT
GAMBLE

FORKS

OLYMPIC
NATIONAL
PARK

BRINNON

OLYMPIC
NATIONAL
FOREST

QUINALT

PACIFIC
OCEAN

N.
↑

Washington's upper Olympic Peninsula is a land of majestic snowcapped peaks, icy glaciers, mountain meadows overflowing with wildflowers, picturesque river valleys, crystal blue lakes and lots of ocean beachfront. Ferry service from Victoria, B.C. calls at **Port Angeles** year round. This city's busy harbor is protected by a natural sandspit that is home to the Coast Guard air rescue station, a public boat launch and picnic facilities.

To reach **Ediz Hook Sand Spit** take Marine Drive east out of Port Angeles, and proceed through the Crown Zellerbach mill grounds. This is a great spot to watch fishing boats come and go and provides a delightful view of the city against its backdrop of mountains. If you were to head west on Marine Drive instead, you would soon arrive at the Port of Port Angeles, this is a good place to watch large freighters as they load and unload their cargo of logs, lumber and other forest products.

Downtown Port Angeles has a very nice **municipal pier and marine laboratory**. It offers an observation tower, promenade decks, a picnic area, short-term moorage, a sandy wading beach, grassy areas for sun bathing and the Arthur D. Fiero Marine Laboratory. The lab displays local marine life and is open Tuesdays and Thursdays from 10:00 a.m. to noon, and weekends between noon and 4:00 p.m.

The **Clallam County Courthouse Museum** is at Lincoln and Fourth. The building is distinctive and easy to spot. It is housed in the 1914 county courthouse, on the second floor. This beautiful building sports a stained glass skylight, marble steps and a clock tower. The museum is devoted to early Clallam County and its pioneers. It is open year round, weekends too during the summer.

You will find an authentic **Indian long house** and a collection of pioneer cabins at Lincoln Park. The park is located on West Lauridsen at Bean Road. Tennis courts, play fields, nature trails and a picnic area are also available.

Port Angeles is also home to the **Olympic National Park Visitors Center**. The Olympic National Park protects the lush rainforest and unspoiled seacoast of Northwest Washington. Still other areas on the peninsula are protected by the Olympic National Forest. At the visitors center on Race Street you can get personal help in choosing the area or trail just right for your skills. One short trail begins right at the west end of the parking lot and takes you past moss hung trees, sparkling pools and moss carpeted rocks.

Inside the center you will find the **Pioneer Memorial Museum** which features displays on wildlife, plantlife and geological aspects of the park. It also includes exhibits depicting an early logging camp and an assortment of Indian whaling tools. The visitors center is open 8:00 a.m. to 4:00 p.m. year round. During the summer they are open until 7:00 p.m.

For a panoramic view of the Strait of Juan de Fuca and Vancouver Island, head south out of Port Angeles to **Hurricane Ridge**. It's 18 miles from town along a good road. The ridge is situated 5,200 feet above sea level and is one of the Olympic National Park's most scenic areas. You will find the view terrific, right from your car. Hiking trails will take you to more viewpoints. Besides the view, you'll find a year round lodge, naturalist walks, park orientation talks, possible wildlife sightings, and all kinds of outdoor activities.

Fishing is one of the most popular activities around Port Angeles. Fishing charters are readily available and come complete with all the necessary equipment. The Peninsula also offers an abundance of freshwater fishing in its many streams, rivers and mountain lakes. Lakes Crescent, Sutherland and Aldwell, as well as the Elwha River, contain many different species of trout.

The **Salt Creek Recreation Area** is 10 miles west of Port Angeles. This land was purchased by Clallam County in 1958. The scenery is beautiful and the rocky point provides a terrific spot for watching the sun set. Fall and spring bring large numbers of waterbirds to the area. Many winter here.

This land was first inhabited by settlers in the 1860's. A cedar shake mill was in operation at Salt Creek in 1915 and another in 1941. Camp Hayden was built here, on Tongue Point, and equipped with a 16 inch gun. Along with the guns at Forts Ebey, Flagler, Casey and Worden it provided protection for Port Angeles, Admiralty Inlet, Port Townsend and the Bremerton harbor.

Lake Crescent is 20 miles west of Port Angeles along US 101. This is one of the area's more spectacular sights, a deep blue lake, surrounded by gentle wooded hills and towering mountains. It reaches more than 600 feet in depth. The lake is glacier fed and harbors large Crescenti and Beardslee trout, two fish unique to this area. Hiking trails lead to the 90 foot Marymere Falls and up Storm King Mountain. Two lodges provide lakeside accommodations.

At the west end of the lake take the road south to **Sol Duc Hot Springs**. This is another area of great beauty and the result of the region's volcanic beginnings. It once was the site of a spa popular with the very wealthy. That spa burned down in 1916. A new lodge and cabins plus two hot sulphur pools make it a favored spot for relaxing while on vacation.

One of the best places for hikers who want to experience the Olympic National Park's unspoiled seacoast is at **Lake Ozette**. To get there follow Highway 112 when it leaves US 101 west of Port Angeles. After 48 miles, take the road to Ozette. Lake Ozette is Washington's third largest lake. This area offers some excellent hiking trails. They will lead you

through deep forests and open prairie to the Pacific Ocean and Cape Alava. This is where the archeological digs of the ancient Ozette Indian village are.

Cape Alava is the most westerly point in the continental United States. The views and undisturbed tide pools found here, are incomparable. This is an excellent starting point for hiking the coastal portion of the Olympic National Park. These are some of the last wilderness beaches on the continental U.S. To the north you will find Point of Arches, a relatively isolated shoreline that is listed on the National Registry of Natural Landmarks because of its beautiful sea sculpted shoreline. To the south, you could hike for days and never tire of the view.

The **Olympic National Forest** is noted for its lush rain forests, Roosevelt elk, rugged mountain terrain, glaciers and permanent mountain snowfields. Nearly 200 miles of trails crisscross its land, some permit horses and motor bikes. You'll find a ranger station at Forks. They will prove helpful in choosing a trail.

Northeast of **Forks**, the **Pioneer's Path Nature Trail** offers a .25 mile loop trail through a forest carpeted with moss. Interpretive signs relate man's past activities here. To find the trail leave US 101 1.7 miles north of Forks on Forest Service Road #300. Head east 5.4 miles to the trailhead.

The road leading westward, to **La Push**, is a good one to follow in the spring. It leads you to the Pacific Ocean and a great spot to watch for migrating whales. They are often sighted here offshore.

The **Hoh-Clearwater Recreation Area** is managed by the Department of Natural Resources. The primary use of this land is for timber production but fishing enthusiasts, campers and hikers are welcome too. This area's northern border is near the town of Forks, the souther border near Queets. You'll find eight free campgrounds and an abundance of trails within its boundaries.

The **Hoh Rain Forest**, south of Forks, averages 145 inches of rain each year. Giant spruce trees 300 foot tall and draped with moss grow here. The area is also said to have the largest variety of wild mushrooms in the continental United States.

The Bogachiel River is famous for its steelhead and salmon fishing. The 118 acre **Bogachiel State Park**, 6 miles south of Forks, provides an excellent place to try the river. Picnic and kitchen facilities are available.

At **Quinault Lake** you'll find sparkling water surrounded by steep mountains, all in a temperate rain forest. This large, low elevation lake has one shore in the Olympic National Forest, the other in the Olympic National Park. During the 1880's a log hotel was built here. It burned down in the early 1920's. A newer, alpine-style lodge which kept the old fashioned touches, but added all the latest in modern conveniences now stands near the shore.

The land that lies to the southwest is part of the Quinault Indian Reservation. Public use of the lake is regulated by the Quinault Tribal Council. Check at the **Quinault** ranger station for current regulations. They can also direct you to local trails like Colonel Bob, which leads to a 4,492 foot summit offering views of Quinault Lake, Mt. Olympus and the Pacific Ocean.

The **Big Tree Grove Nature Trail** is a short loop through a magnificent stand of centuries old Douglas fir. Signs along the way explain the features of the area. This is the Quinault Rain Forest, a natural greenhouse. Each year approximately twelve feet of rain falls in this area. The warm, humid climate produces a variety of plants, ferns and hanging mosses. Watch for directional signs to the Big Tree Grove Trail just outside Quinault.

If you head east on US 101 out of Port Angeles, and follow Kitchen Road north through Dungeness County Park, you'll soon come to the **Dungeness National Wildlife Refuge**. The calm waters of Dungeness Bay make this an outstanding area for watching shorebirds. This is also a key wintering and spring gathering place for black brant and other migrating waterfowl. An occasional killer whale, along with other marine mammals, is spotted here as well.

At **Sequim**, 15 miles east of Port Angeles, you can visit the **Sequim-Dungeness Museum**. Their displays include scale model lighthouses, ship models, mastodon artifacts, marine specimens and a variety of historical exhibits. They are open Tuesday thru Sunday from mid-May to November, between noon and 4:00 p.m. The balance of the year they are open Wednesdays, Fridays and Saturdays only. You'll find the museum at 175 West Cedar.

Visitors to **The Manis Mastodon Site** are treading on land where the earliest evidence of man's presence in the Pacific Northwest has been found. It is also the only place in all of

North America where certain evidence that humans hunted and butchered mastodons has been unearthed. Excavations are being done by a team of archaeologists from Washington State University.

In 1977 the owner of this land, Emanual Manis, was digging a pond in his ten-acre front yard. A few feet beneath the ground he pried loose the first in a succession of mastodon tusks and bones. Digs are conducted here throughout the summer. Visitors are welcome from the end of June thru Labor Day. You will be treated to a slide show describing the discovery of the mastodon skeleton and a chance to view the excavations. To get there leave US 101 on 3rd Avenue. Turn right on Happy Valley Road, left on McFarland Road and left again onto the site.

The **Sequim Bay Recreation Area** is located 4 miles east of town. It sits in the protective rain shadow of the Olympic Mountains and only receives between 10 and 15 inches of rain per year, one tenth of what the rain forests west of here receive. Facilities include a boat launch, mooring buoys and floats, kitchen facilities and picnic shelters.

At the **Olympic Game Farm** you'll find a number of retired animal movie stars remembered for their roles in major wildlife movies and tv series. The farm offers both drive through and guided walking tours. Besides observing wild animals at close range, you'll be treated to a live bear performance and animal petting area.

Historic and picturesque **Port Townsend** contains the best collection of Victorian architecture north of San Francisco. Two Victorian Homes Tours are held each year, one on the first weekend in May and the other the third weekend in September. The balance of the year you can easily make your own **historic home tour**, although you will only be able to study the outsides.

A map showing the exact locations and history of Port Townsend homes and buildings is available at the local Chamber of Commerce office. It will help you to find the 1865 St. Paul's Episcopal Church, 1893 Customs House, 1889 Hastings

Building, 1874 Fowler Building, dozens of historic homes and mansions plus other historic sites. Both the downtown Port Townsend waterfront district, and the residential area on the bluff, have been designated National Historic Districts.

Port Townsend was a bustling seaport prior to the turn of the century. With the coming of the railroad, Seattle became the seaport metropolis Port Townsend had longed to become, and Port Townsend was left to sleep for many decades. Today the majority of the town's gracious mansions, built between 1860 and the turn of the century, have been restored. Many serve the tourist industry.

The elegant **Rothschild House** was built in 1868 by an early Port Townsend merchant. It is currently maintained by the State Parks and Recreation Commission and may be toured daily, from April 15th thru October 15th, between 10:00 a.m. and 5:00 p.m. It is open weekends and holidays only during the balance of the year, between 11:00 a.m. and 4:00 p.m. The house is situated at Franklin and Taylor.

You'll find the **Jefferson County Historical Museum** on the ground floor of the City Hall Building, at Madison and Water Streets. The building was erected in 1891. Inside, historic memorabilia, antiques and photographs provide insight into Port Townsend's early days. The museum is open Thursday thru Monday, year round, between 10:45 a.m. and 3:45 p.m.

Situated at the tip of the peninsula, Fort Worden was built around 1897 to help protect Puget Sound from enemy invasion. It was closed by the military, after the Korean War. The land and buildings are now part of the **Fort Worden State Park**. The 330 acre estate features a collection of restored Victorian officer's houses, barracks, parade grounds and artillery bunkers. Special features include abandoned gun emplacements and the U.S. Government Cemetery. The commanding officer's quarters is open for tours daily, 10:00 a.m. to 5:00 p.m., May thru September.

A public boat launch, fishing, swimming, mooring buoys and floats, scuba diving, hiking, beachcombing, kitchen facilities and picnic tables can be enjoyed within the park, plus there's a lighthouse on the point. Vacationers can also rent the Victorian style officers' row houses.

Established in 1859, **Old Fort Townsend** protected the surrounding area in case of Indian uprisings, until 1895. Today a state park protects the historic fort and its surrounding 377 acres. Picnic shelters, 7 miles of hiking trails, beach access and fishing can all be enjoyed here. The old fort is east of Highway 20, 3 miles south of Port Townsend.

To reach **Fort Flagler State Park**, leave Port Townsend on Highway 20 and head east on the road to Hadlock and Marrowstone Island. The fort is located at the northern end of Marrowstone Island. You can tour the grounds, explore some of the park's 793 acres, walk the beaches, go clamming, crabbing or fishing. A boat launch, mooring buoys and floats, kitchen facilities and picnic tables are there too. This former fort was also established in the 1850's.

Eaglemont Rockeries is the product of one woman and her family. What started as a simple yard decoration in 1948, now covers much of the property. Stones, concrete and driftwood have been transformed into castles, towns, various scenes, animals, pioneers, an Indian village, and a long list of other items. The rockery is located near the junction of Highway 20 and Old 104, south of Port Townsend.

You can take Highway 104 to **Port Gamble** as well. In 1853, Captain William Talbot established here, what is today considered to be the oldest continuously operating sawmill in North America. The surrounding community sports an unusual New England architectural style. The Pope & Talbot Lumber Company, who owns this company town, has restored it to look like it did when Talbot's town was new, at the turn of the century. The entire town has been designated a **National Historic Site**.

Main Street offers the 1853 U.S. Post Office, 1870 Masonic Temple, 1870 Episcopal Church and some beautifully restored 19th century homes. The Thompson House, built in 1859, is the oldest continuously occupied house in the state. Other community highlights include the restored General Store and the sawmill itself.

The **Pope & Talbot Historical Museum** is located on the downhill side of the Port Gamble General Store. The exhibits seen here trace the history of the founders of Pope & Talbot, who left their homes and businesses in Maine more than 125 years ago to test their strengths and skills against an untamed West. The museum is open daily throughout the summer between 10:00 a.m. and 12:00 noon and 1:00 p.m. and 4:00 p.m.

You'll find shells and marine life on exhibit at the **Of Sea and Shore Museum**. This exceptional collection was put together by Tom Rice, a Port Gamble native and editor of an international magazine for shell collectors. It contains more than 14,000 species of mollusks (shells) and several thousand specimens of other marine life. The museum's summer hours are Tuesday thru Friday, 12:00 noon to 4:00 p.m., Saturday and Sunday from 12:00 noon to 6:00 p.m.

Back on U.S. 101, if you head south towards **Quilcene**, you can visit a **fish hatchery** where 25 million salmon eggs are produced each year. You will find both a visitors center and an aquarium at this location. Visitors are welcome, year round, between 8:00 a.m. and 4:00 p.m.

A little farther south, 2 miles before you reach **Brinnon**, you will come upon **Seal Rock Beach**. At first glance, this setting appears quiet. Upon closer examination, you will see that it's teeming with activity. This typical Puget Sound beach features tiny purple shore crabs, gulls, great blue herons, harbor seals and Pacific oysters. When the tide is out, the tidal pools are filled with life. This beach is managed by the Olympic National Forest in hopes that everyone will gain a better understanding of the marine environment.

While Seal Beach is an important habitat for marine flora and fauna, this same beach provides many recreational opportunities. Oyster picking, clam digging, crabbing, scuba diving, swimming and beachcombing are all exciting activities enjoyed here.

Continuing past Brinnon about 1 mile, you'll find **Dosewallips State Park**. This 425 acre recreation area is a favorite with fishing enthusiasts because it offers winter steelhead fishing in the Dosewallips River, and salmon and bottom fishing in Hood Canal. Clams and oysters are also found there. This lovely park offers all of the usual facilities and activities found in Washington state parks.

ACCOMMODATIONS

Whether you're looking for a deluxe resort, modest motel or backpacker's campsite, Washington's northwest corner has it all. One phone call, to the Chamber of Commerce office in the area you wish to visit, will provide you with information on accommodations available. Below is a list of Chamber addresses and phone numbers.

Anacortes Chamber of Commerce
(206)293-3832
1319 Commercial Avenue
Anacortes, WA 98221

Bellevue Chamber of Commerce
(206)454-2464
110-116th SE #10
Bellevue, WA 98005

Bellingham/Whatcom County
Vistors & Convention Bureau
(206)671-3990
1224 Cornwall Avenue
Bellingham, WA 98227

Blaine Community Chamber of Commerce
(206)332-6025
P.O. Box 1718
Blaine, WA 98230

Burlington Chamber of Commerce
(206)755-9260
701 Fairhaven Avenue
Burlington, WA 98233

Central Whidbey Island Chamber of Commerce
(206)678-4066
P.O. Box 152
Coupeville, WA 98239

Concrete Chamber of Commerce
(206)853-8181
P.O. Box 12
Concrete, WA 98237

Everett Area Chamber of Commerce
(206)252-5107
P.O. Box 1086
Everett, WA 98206

Ferndale Chamber of Commerce
(206)384-3042
P.O. Box 300
Ferndale, WA 98248

Forks Chamber of Commerce
(206)374-2531
P.O. Box 300
Forks, WA 98331

La Conner Chamber of Commerce
(206)354-5995
P.O. Box 644
La Conner, WA 98257

Lynden Chamber of Commerce
(206)354-3675
P.O. Box 647
Lynden, WA 98264

Marysville Chamber of Commerce
(206)659-7700
P.O. Box 151
Marysville, WA 98270

Mt. Vernon Chamber of Commerce
(206)336-9555
516 S. 2nd Street
Mt. Vernon, WA 98273

Orcas Island Chamber of Commerce
(206)376-2273
P.O. Box 252
Eastsound, WA 98245

Port Angeles Chamber of Commerce
(206)452-2363
1217 East 1st Street
Port Angeles, WA 98362

Port Townsend Chamber of Commerce
(206)385-2722
2437 Sims Way
Port Townsend, WA 98368

San Juan Island Chamber of Commerce
(206)378-5240
P.O. Box 98
Friday Harbor, WA 98250

Seattle/King County
Convention & Visitors Center
(206)447-4240
666 Stewart St.
Seattle, WA 98101

Sedro Woolley Chamber of Commerce
(206)855-0770
714 Metcalf Street
Sedro Woolley, WA 98284

Snohomish Chamber of Commerce
(206)568-2526
118 Avenue B
Snohomish, WA 98290

If you've enjoyed **WASHINGTON IN YOUR POCKET**, you may want to purchase additional Ki² books and discover more of the Pacific Northwest's leisure time attractions.

Our two current best sellers are **OREGON FREE, A GUIDE TO THE BEST OF THE STATE'S COST FREE ATTRACTIONS** and its companion volume **WASHINGTON FREE**. Together they will show you where to find nearly 2500 fun, free places to go.

With these two guidebooks you can explore the Pacific Northwest's ghost towns, covered bridges, historic sites, museums, parks and public lands, bicycle paths, hot springs, hiking trails, scenic areas, natural wonders, caves, rockhouding spots, waterfalls, art collections, wildlife refuges and more!

The books are set up in an easy to use manner and include brief descriptions of each free attraction as well as directions and schedules where necessary. Easy to read maps, a detailed table of contents plus a thorough index make them a breeze to use. Anyone who loves the Pacific Northwest will love these books!

FREE CAMPGROUNDS OF WASHINGTON & OREGON is perfect for those of you who enjoy camping away from concrete slabs and civilization. It will show you exactly where to find the two state's more than 600 cost free campgrounds. Listings cover the facilities available at each campground and give precise, easy to follow directions. The index highlights where you will find campsites designated for tents only, those with rv access and what length trailer will fit plus which sites offer fishing, hiking trails, horse facilities, a boat launch and more.

All Ki² books carry a moneyback guarantee when returned in saleable condition, within 10 days of purchase.

MAILORDER COUPONS

✂ ---

Please send me the following books:

___ WASHINGTON IN YOUR POCKET @ $4.95 ea _____
___ WASHINGTON FREE @ $9.95 ea _____
___ FREE CAMPGROUNDS OF WA & OR @ $5.95 ea_____
___ OREGON FREE @ $9.95 ea _____
___ OR/WA HIGHWAY MAP @ $1.00 ea _____
    Please add $1 per book ($3 max) for shipping _____
                            TOTAL $_____

Name_____
Address_____
City/State/Zip Code_____

Send this order coupon to Ki² Enterprises, P.O. Box 13322, Portland, Oregon 97213.

✂ ---

Please send me the following books:

___WASHINGTON IN YOUR POCKET @ $4.95 ea _____
___WASHINGTON FREE @ $9.95 ea _____
___FREE CAMPGROUNDS OF WA & OR @ $5.95 ea_____
___OREGON FREE @ $9.95 ea _____
___OR/WA HIGHWAY MAP @ $1.00 ea _____
    Please add $1 per book ($3 max) for shipping _____
                            TOTAL $_____

Name_____
Address_____
City/State/Zip Code_____

Send this order coupon to Ki² Enterprises, P.O. Box 13322, Portland, Oregon 97213.

INDEX